Cats! Cats! Cats!

Cats! Cats! Cats!

A Loving Look

At Those Fabulous Felines

Edited by

Mary Alice Loberg

Beautifully Illustrated

With Artwork and Photographs

 HALLMARK EDITIONS

INTRODUCTION

I am a cat lover. I have owned, fed, rescued, nursed, midwifed, loved, and buried more fabulous felines than I can remember. I have argued their worth to dog lovers and defended their right to hunt birds to bird lovers. I have written about them, studied them and found them to be the most interesting of all animals. And so it was a great personal delight to collect and select the prose and poetry for this book.

It is my belief that those who think they do not like cats should open up and admit their vulnerability. On many occasions I have known cats to work their way into the homes and hearts of those who at one time said, "No, I don't like cats." These people have found that each individual cat differs in many ways from each other individual cat. Just as people differ.

It has been said that cats prefer places to people. Some do. They have been known to travel hundreds of miles to return to homes from which they have been removed. But thousands more move with their families every year, adjusting quickly to their new environment.

Some people complain that cats are sneaky and

silent. Some are. But I have known cats who stumble, fall, and walk across a wooden floor with as much stealth as a Clydesdale.

Many people have said that cats are cold and unaffectionate. Some are. Others have all the enthusiasm, warmth, and friendliness of the most devoted dog.

Some cats panic at the sight of water. Others have been known to willfully subject themselves to a bath once a week. Some cats are finicky in their eating habits, requiring the tenderest filets and the sweetest cream. Others are content with mice, grasshoppers, and macaroni and cheese.

I mention all of this only to emphasize the need to accept each cat as an individual, in the same way that we should accept people.

I know that I cannot convert all readers into the great ranks of cat lovers. I wish I could. But the best that I can hope is that everyone will have as good a time reading this book as I had compiling it.

—MARY ALICE LOBERG

Cats! Cats! Cats!

THE CAT

The age-old cat lover vs. dog lover argument
comes to life in this interesting comparison
by William Lyon Phelps.

The cat is the most beautiful and graceful of all domestic animals. His anatomy is precisely adapted to his needs; and although he takes only a hundredth as much exercise as a dog, he is always in perfect condition . . . . There is no other beast who from a position of absolute relaxation can spring with accuracy and with no preliminary motion. He does not have to wind up like a baseball pitcher, or get "set"; he transmutes potential into kinetic energy with no visible effort, no more than a king-fisher's, only, instead of falling like the halcyon, he rises.

When a cat aims at the top of a fence or the surface of a table, he usually succeeds at the first attempt, unlike the dog, who tries five or six times and continues to try after the impossibility of attainment has been clearly demonstrated. The cat's economy of effort is as remarkable as his judgment of distance; you cannot persuade him to try for any mark manifestly beyond his reach. The cat catches birds on the ground by outguessing them, and then by a motion swifter than wings; but if the bird rises in the air, the cat makes no attempt at pursuit, which he knows to be futile and undignified; the dog, on the other hand, will chase after flying birds so long as he is able to run, although the percentage of hits is zero.

FUN

His amiable amber eyes
Are very friendly, very wise;
Like Buddha, grave and fat,
He sits, regardless of applause,
And thinking, as he kneads his paws,
What fun to be a cat!

—CHRISTOPHER MORLEY

THE WAY OF A CAT

When first I saw you at my door,
A homeless kitten, starved and poor,
Your eyes were very scared and wide —
You hardly dared to come inside.
But afterward when you had dined,
You grew quite happily resigned;
Much like a child you sought my lap
And snuggled down to take a nap.
Time passed and you became quite gay
And played and romped the livelong day.
But all too quickly you outgrew
The spool and string I gave to you,
And went on weird, nocturnal jaunts —
Dark alleys were your favorite haunts.
And now that you are worldly wise,
You sit aloof with half-closed eyes,
And scarcely ever pay much heed
To me, except in time of need.
And then you softly purr and raise
Your eyes to mine in pleading gaze
For plates of cream and bits of meat,
(I fear, at times, you show deceit,)
Some say you are a hypocrite,
I love you though, in spite of it.

—MARGARET E. BRUNER

THE TOM CAT

At midnight in the alley
    A tomcat comes to wail,
And he chants the hate of a million years
    As he swings his snaky tail.

He will lie on a rug tomorrow
    And lick his silky fur,
And veil the brute in his yellow eyes
    And play he's tame, and purr.

But at midnight in the alley
    He will crouch again and wail,
And beat the time for demon's song
    With the swing of his demon's tail.

—DON MARQUIS

APPETITE

Let take a cat, and foster him well with milk
And tender flesh, and make his couch of silk,
And let him see a mouse go by the wall,
Anon he waveth milk, and flesh, and all,
And every dainty which is in that house,
Such appetite hath he to eat a mouse.

—GEOFFREY CHAUCER

THE AUTOMOBILE AND THE CAT

Whose little lanterns are these
so close to the road, so bright?
Two little green lanterns that shine
back at our great headlight?
Something is walking alone,
alone through the lonely night,
something little which carries
two green flames for a light.

—ELIZABETH COATSWORTH

THE RULE

There is a rule about cats: if you have only one cat,
you become a cat. The universe is the cat and you,
and the cat does not differentiate. If you have two
cats, they relate primarily to each other. If you
have three or more, I think you don't exist at all.
The cats become a tribe unto themselves.

—DAVID MC REYNOLDS

KITTEN UP A TREE

A pole! A ladder! Anything!
    Arouse the sleepy town!
Oh, who is brave enough to bring
    The frightened kitten down?

Enamored of the moving shade
    And for the giddy leaf,
How could she know a clever maid
    So soon might come to grief?

We saw her mount the bough
    At her fastidious ease.
And there was none to tell her how
    Inexorable are trees,

As up the slippery avenue
    She delicately went,
Occasionally pausing to
    Admire her own ascent.

And now she shivers on a limb.
    Her little claws are blunted,
And helpless pussy by two grim
    Finalities confronted.

The tossing branch will not be still;
    The trunk is dead and steep.
For going back she has no skill,
    No courage for the leap.

A ladder quickly! Someone come!
    We lose the dwindling light.
Ah, who will save a kitten from
    This most atrocious plight?
            —PHYLLIS MC GINLEY

BAST

She had green eyes, that excellent seer,
And little peaks to either ear.
She sat there, and I sat here.

She spoke of Egypt, and a white
Temple, against enormous night.

She smiled with clicking teeth and said
That the dead were never dead;

Said old emperors hang like bats
In barns at night, or ran like rats —
But empresses came back as cats!
            —WILLIAM ROSE BENÉT

THE RADICAL CAT
*The similarities between radicals and cats
are explained by William Kunstler
in an article titled "The Centrality of the Cat."*

Cats are radical in this sense: they share the attributes of most radical people. First of all, they're aloof. They have a loneliness about them. A cat can live with solitude if there are no people around. Cats have a certain reserve in giving their affection; they give it only when they desire to, and it can't be coaxed out of them. Secondly, they're independent. They can support themselves and keep themselves alive. A cat adapts very quickly to his surroundings and learns how to blend with the landscape; in other words, a cat can go underground. Thirdly, they're secretive. They know how to come and go in silence — unlike dogs, who bark constantly. Fourthly, they know how to defend themselves. They are sensitive, and instantly alert. Cats have a battery of weapons. And they know a great deal about infighting. Lastly, you can't make a cat conform as you can a dog. A cat will never beg for food, or roll over and play dead, or do tricks or other slavish things. Cats have a great dignity about them that dogs lack. A dog is like a liberal. He wants to please everybody. A cat doesn't really need to know that everybody loves him.

A TOM CAT AGING

The old tom cat sits by the fire
   licking his curled up paws,
blinking in quiet contentment,
   stretching his whiskered jaws . . .

The years have been favorable to him.
   He still has his well-groomed fur;
his eyesight's as keen as ever;
   he still has his masculine purr . . .

And yet there is one thing that plagues him,
   he's noticed it once or twice . . .
time has been gradually breeding
   a speedier race of mice.

              —MARY ALICE LOBERG

THE BATH

His tongue is sponge, and brush, and towel, and
    curry-comb,
Well he knows what work it can be made to do,
Poor little wash-rag, smaller than my thumb.

His nose touches his back, touches his hind paws
    too,
Every patch of fur is raked, and scraped, and
    smoothed;
What more has Goethe done, what more could
    Voltaire do?

—HIPPOLYTE TAINE

CLIMBING

Another side of the cat's fascinating character
is discussed by Dr. Louis J. Camuti,
a New York City veterinarian,
in his book Park Avenue Vet.

The cat's gracefulness has inspired dancers, paint-
ers, and poets. Cats have also acquired the reputa-
tion of being sure-footed, always poised, but do
they deserve it? Well, most of the time. Any tree-
climbing animal is relatively sure-footed. But cats
have their clumsy moments when they slip, slide,
lose their balance, misjudge distances, and act like
complete amateurs in the art of catlike behavior.

Cats are supposed to be able to jump to a table
without first seeing what's on it, and orient themselves so quickly that nothing is disturbed. This is
true, I've seen them do it. I've also seen cats jump
onto tables and fall into soup bowls, knock over
salt shakers, and send the silverware flying before
getting their bearings. Cats climb trees, then wonder how to get down again. The reason for this is
simple. A cat's claws curve forward and this allows
him to climb up very easily. But if he wants to
climb down, he has to do it backwards; otherwise,
his curved claws wouldn't grip. This is a difficult
maneuver and many cats forget just how difficult
it is until they try to do it. Then they get scared

and panicky, and so do their owners. (Don't worry. In most cases, the cat will figure things out for himself, faster and better than his human assistants.)

Cats go to sleep on chairs, wake up, stretch — and fall off. They do the same thing on window sills. It happens so often that I always advise owners to screen their windows. Otherwise, the graceful, sure-footed cat will ignominiously tumble out. It's true that cats land on their feet, but even a short drop may be fatal. I know of several cats who suffered broken spines or legs in a mere five-foot fall. Others have been luckier.

One owner called to tell me that her Siamese had just fallen from her apartment window to the street, eight floors below.

"I'm afraid it's too late," I said. "I'm sorry. There's not much I can do."

"What do you mean?" cried the woman. "The cat's trying to climb up the side of the building!"

"Still alive?" I asked in amazement.

"She's not only alive," the woman said, "she's mad as hell!"

When I examined the Siamese later, I found her in perfect shape. Indignant, furious, embarrassed, and extremely vocal, but otherwise unhurt. There was one slight inconvenience; she had chipped a front tooth.

The Cat That Walked By Himself

Hear and attend and listen; for this befell and behappened and became and was, O my Best Beloved, when the animals were wild. The Dog was wild, and the Horse was wild, and the Pig was wild — as wild as wild could be — and they walked in the Wet Wild Woods by their wild lones. But the wildest of all the wild animals was the Cat. He walked by himself, and all places were alike to him.

Of course the Man was wild too. He was dreadfully wild. He didn't even begin to be tame till he met the Woman, and she told him that she did not like living in his wild ways. She picked out a nice dry Cave, instead of a heap of wet leaves, to lie down in; and she strewed clean sand on the floor; and she lit a nice fire of wood at the back of the Cave; and she hung a dried wild-horse skin, tail-down, across the opening of the Cave; and she said, "Wipe your feet, dear, when you come in, and now we'll keep house."

That night, Best Beloved, they ate wild sheep roasted on the hot stones, and flavoured with wild garlic and wild pepper; and wild duck stuffed with wild rice and wild fenugreek and wild coriander; and marrow-bones of wild oxen; and wild cherries, and wild grenadillas. Then the Man went to sleep in front of the fire ever so happy; but the Woman sat up, combing her hair. She took the bone of the shoulder of mutton — the big fat blade-bone — and she looked at the wonderful marks on it, and she threw more wood on the fire, and she made a Magic. She made the First Singing Magic in the world.

Out in the Wet Wild Woods all the wild animals gathered together where they could see the light of the fire a long way off, and they wondered what it meant.

Then Wild Horse stamped with his wild foot and said, "O my Friends and O my Enemies, why have the Man and the Woman made that great light in that great Cave, and what harm will it do us?"

Wild Dog lifted up his wild nose and smelled the smell of roast mutton, and said, "I will go up and see and look, and say; for I think it is good. Cat, come with me."

"Nenni!" said the Cat. "I am the Cat who walks by himself, and all places are alike to me. I will not come."

"Then we can never be friends again," said Wild Dog, and he trotted off to the Cave. But when he had gone a little way the Cat said to himself, "All places are alike to me. Why should I not go too and see and look and come away at my own liking." So he slipped after Wild Dog softly, very softly, and hid himself where he could hear everything.

When Wild Dog reached the mouth of the Cave he lifted up the dried horse-skin with his nose and sniffed the beautiful smell of the roast mutton, and the Woman, looking at the blade-bone, heard him, and laughed, and said, "Here comes the first. Wild Thing out of the Wild Woods, what do you want?"

Wild Dog said, "O my Enemy and Wife of my Enemy, what is this that smells so good in the Wild Woods?"

Then the Woman picked up a roasted mutton-bone and threw it to Wild Dog, and said, "Wild Thing out of the Wild Woods, taste and try." Wild Dog gnawed the bone, and it was more delicious than anything he had ever tasted, and he said, "O my Enemy and Wife of my Enemy, give me another."

The Woman said, "Wild Thing out of the Wild Woods, help my Man to hunt through the day and guard this Cave at night, and I will give you as many roast bones as you need."

"Ah!" said the Cat, listening. "This is a very wise Woman, but she is not so wise as I am."

Wild Dog crawled into the Cave and laid his head on the Woman's lap, and said, "O my Friend and Wife of my Friend, I will help your Man to hunt through the day, and at night I will guard your Cave."

"Ah!" said the Cat, listening. "That is a very foolish Dog." And he went back through the Wet Wild Woods waving his wild tail, and walking by his wild lone. But he never told anybody.

When the Man waked up he said, "What is Wild Dog doing here?" And the Woman said, "His name is not Wild Dog any more, but the First Friend, because he will be our friend for always and always and always. Take him with you when you go hunting." . . .

The next night the Cat watched Wild Horse become First Servant in exchange for fresh green grass prepared by Woman. Likewise on the third night Wild Cow agreed to become the Giver of Food in return for three daily meals of the wonderful grass.

Next day the Cat waited to see if any other Wild thing would go up to the Cave, but no one moved in the Wet Wild Woods, so the Cat walked there by himself; and he saw the Woman milking the Cow, and he saw the light of the fire in the Cave, and he smelt the smell of warm white milk.

Cat said, "O my Enemy and Wife of my Enemy, where did Wild Cow go?"

The Woman laughed and said, "Wild Thing out of the Wild Woods, go back to the Woods again, for I have braided up my hair, and I have put away the magic blade-bone, and we have no more need of either friends or servants in our Cave."

Cat said, "I am not a friend, and I am not a

24

servant. I am the Cat who walks by himself, and I wish to come into your cave."

Woman said, "Then why did you not come with First Friend on the first night?"

Cat grew very angry and said, "Has Wild Dog told tales of me?"

Then the Woman laughed and said, "You are the Cat who walks by himself, and all places are alike to you. You are neither a friend nor a servant. You have said it yourself. Go away and walk by yourself in all places alike."

Then Cat pretended to be sorry and said, "Must I never come into the Cave? Must I never sit by the warm fire? Must I never drink the warm white milk? You are very wise and very beautiful. You should not be cruel even to a Cat."

Woman said, "I knew I was wise, but I did not know I was beautiful. So I will make a bargain with you. If ever I say one word in your praise you may come into the Cave."

"And if you say two words in my praise?" said the Cat.

"I never shall," said the Woman, "but if I say two words in your praise, you may sit by the fire in the Cave."

"And if you say three words?" said the Cat.

"I never shall," said the Woman, "but if I say three words in your praise, you may drink the warm white milk three times a day for always and always and always."

Then the Cat arched his back and said, "Now let the Curtain at the mouth of the Cave, and the Fire at the back of the Cave, and the Milk-pots that stand beside the Fire, remember what my Enemy and the Wife of my Enemy has said." And he went away through the Wet Wild Woods waving his wild tail and walking by his wild lone.

That night when the Man and the Horse and the Dog came home from hunting, the Woman did not tell them of the bargain that she had made with the Cat, because she was afraid that they might not like it.

Cat went far and far away and hid himself in the Wet Wild Woods by his wild lone for a long time till the Woman forgot all about him. Only the Bat — the little upside-down Bat — that hung inside the Cave, knew where Cat hid; and every evening Bat would fly to Cat with news of what was happening.

One evening Bat said, "There is a Baby in the Cave. He is new and pink and fat and small, and the Woman is very fond of him."

"Ah," said the Cat, listening, "but what is the Baby fond of?"

"He is fond of things that are soft and tickle," said the Bat. "He is fond of warm things to hold in

his arms when he goes to sleep. He is fond of being played with. He is fond of all those things."

"Ah," said the Cat, listening, "then my time has come."

Next night Cat walked through the Wet Wild Woods and hid very near the Cave till morning-time, and Man and Dog and Horse went hunting. The Woman was busy cooking that morning, and the Baby cried and interrupted. So she carried him outside the Cave and gave him a handful of pebbles to play with. But still the Baby cried.

Then the Cat put out his paddy paw and patted the Baby on the cheek, and it cooed; and the Cat rubbed against its fat knees and tickled it under its fat chin with his tail. And the Baby laughed; and the Woman heard him and smiled.

Then the Bat — the little upside-down Bat — that hung in the mouth of the Cave said, "O my Hostess and Wife of my Host and Mother of my Host's Son, a Wild Thing from the Wild Woods is most beautifully playing with your Baby."

"A blessing on that Wild Thing whoever he may be," said the Woman, straightening her back, "for I was a busy woman this morning and he has done me a service."

That very minute and second, Best Beloved, the dried horse-skin Curtain that was stretched tail-down at the mouth of the Cave fell down —

whoosh! — because it remembered the bargain she had made with the Cat, and when the Woman went to pick it up — lo and behold! — the Cat was sitting quite comfy inside the Cave.

"O my Enemy and Wife of my Enemy and Mother of my Enemy," said the Cat, "it is I: for you have spoken a word in my praise, and now I can sit within the Cave for always and always and always. But still I am the Cat who walks by himself, and all places are alike to me."

The Woman was very angry, and shut her lips tight and took up her spinning-wheel and began to spin.

But the Baby cried because the Cat had gone away, and the Woman could not hush it, for it struggled and kicked and grew black in the face.

"O my Enemy and Wife of my Enemy and Mother of my Enemy," said the Cat, "take a strand of the wire that you are spinning and tie it to your spinning-whorl and drag it along the floor, and I will show you a magic that shall make your Baby laugh as loudly as he is now crying."

"I will do so," said the Woman, "because I am at my wits' end; but I will not thank you for it."

She tied the thread to the little clay spindle-whorl and drew it across the floor, and the Cat ran after it and patted it with his paws and rolled head over heels, and tossed it backward over his shoulder and chased it between his hind-legs and pretended to lose it, and pounced down upon it again, till the Baby laughed as loudly as it had been crying, and scrambled after the Cat and frolicked all over the Cave till it grew tired and settled down to sleep with the Cat in its arms.

"Now," said the Cat, "I will sing the Baby a song that shall keep him asleep for an hour." And he began to purr, loud and low, low and loud, till the Baby fell fast asleep. The Woman smiled as she looked down upon the two of them and said, "That was wonderfully done. No question but you are very clever, O Cat."

That very minute and second, Best Beloved, the smoke of the fire at the back of the Cave came down in clouds from the roof — *puff!* — because it remembered the bargain she had made with the Cat, and when it had cleared away — lo and behold — the Cat was sitting quite comfy close to the fire.

"O my Enemy and Wife of my Enemy and Mother of my Enemy," said the Cat, "it is I, for you have spoken a second word in my praise, and now I can sit by the warm fire at the back of the Cave for always and always and always."

Then the Woman was very very angry, and let down her hair and put more wood on the fire and brought out the broad blade-bone of the shoulder of mutton and began to make a Magic that should prevent her from saying a third word in praise of the Cat. It was not a Singing Magic, Best Beloved, it was a Still Magic; and by and by the Cave grew so still that a little wee-wee mouse crept out of a corner and ran across the floor.

"O my Enemy and Wife of my Enemy and Mother of my Enemy," said the Cat, "is that little mouse part of your magic?"

"Ouh! Chee! No indeed!" said the Woman, and she dropped the blade-bone and jumped upon the footstool in front of the fire and braided up her hair very quick for fear that the mouse should run up it.

"Ah," said the Cat, watching, "then the mouse will do me no harm if I eat it?"

"No," said the Woman, braiding up her hair, "eat it quickly and I will ever be grateful to you."

Cat made one jump and caught the little mouse, and the Woman said, "A hundred thanks. Even the First Friend is not quick enough to catch little mice as you have done. You must be very wise."

That very moment and second, O Best Beloved, the Milk-pot that stood by the fire cracked in two pieces — *ffft* — because it remembered the bargain she had made with the Cat, and when the Woman jumped down from the footstool — lo and behold! — the Cat was lapping up the warm white milk that lay in one of the broken pieces.

"O my Enemy and Wife of my Enemy and Mother of my Enemy," said the Cat, "it is I; for you have spoken three words in my praise, and now I can drink the warm white milk three times a day for always and always and always. But *still* I am the Cat who walks by himself, and all places are alike to me."

Then the Woman laughed and set the Cat a bowl of the warm white milk and said, "O Cat, you are as clever as a man, but remember that your bargain was not made with the Man or the Dog, and I do not know what they will do when they come home."

"What is that to me?" said the Cat. "If I have my place in the Cave by the fire and my warm white milk three times a day I do not care what the Man or the Dog can do."

That evening when the Man and the Dog came into the Cave, the Woman told them all the story of the bargain while the Cat sat by the fire and smiled. Then the Man said, "Yes, but he has not made a bargain with *me* or with all proper Men after me." Then he took off his two leather boots and he took up his little stone axe (that makes three) and he fetched a piece of wood and a hatchet (that is five altogether), and he set them out in a row and he said, "Now we will make *our* bargain. If you do not catch mice when you are in the Cave for always and always and always, I will throw these five things at you whenever I see you, and so shall all proper Men do after me."

"Ah," said the Woman, listening, "this is a very clever Cat, but he is not so clever as my Man."

The Cat counted the five things (and they looked very knobby) and he said, "I will catch mice when I am in the Cave for always and always and always; but *still* I am the Cat who walks by himself, and all places are alike to me."

"Not when I am near," said the Man. "If you had not said that last I would have put all these things away for always and always and always; but I am now going to throw my two boots and my little stone axe (that makes three) at you whenever I meet you. And so shall all proper Men after me!"

Then the Dog said, "Wait a minute. He has not made a bargain with *me* or with all proper Dogs after me." And he showed his teeth and said, "If you are not kind to the Baby while I am in the Cave for always and always and always, I will hunt you till I catch you, and when I catch you I will bite you. And so shall all proper Dogs do after me."

"Ah," said the Woman, listening, "this is a very clever Cat, but he is not so clever as the Dog."

Cat counted the Dog's teeth (and they looked very pointed) and he said, "I will be kind to the

Baby while I am in the Cave, as long as he does not pull my tail too hard, for always and always and always. But *still* I am the Cat that walks by himself, and all places are alike to me."

"Not when I am near," said the Dog. "If you had not said that last I would have shut my mouth for always and always and always; but *now* I am going to hunt you up a tree whenever I meet you. And so shall all proper Dogs do after me."

Then the Man threw his two boots and his little stone axe (that makes three) at the Cat, and the Cat ran out of the Cave and the Dog chased him up a tree; and from that day to this, Best Beloved, three proper Men out of five will always throw things at a Cat whenever they meet him, and all proper Dogs will chase him up a tree. But the Cat keeps his side of the bargain too. He will kill mice and he will be kind to Babies when he is in the house, just as long as they do not pull his tail too hard. But when he has done that, and between times, and when the moon gets up and night comes, he is the Cat that walks by himself, and all places are alike to him. Then he goes out to the Wet Wild Woods or up the Wet Wild Trees or on the Wet Wild Roofs, waving his wild tail and walking by his wild lone.

—RUDYARD KIPLING
from "Just So Stories"

from BLACK CAT

All glances that upon her fall she keeps
within herself, to hide thus and to hold,
over them threatening, annoyed at last,
shivering — and then — and then she sleeps.
But turning suddenly as if awaked,
her face directly fronts upon your own:
and there you meet your own glance in the gold
amber of her widened round eye-stone
unexpectedly again: enclosed, held fast,
like an insect long ago extinct.

—RAINER MARIA RILKE

SHE SIGHTS A BIRD

She sights a bird, she chuckles,
She flattens, then she crawls,
She runs without the look of feet,
Her eyes increase to balls,

Her jaws stir, twitching, hungry,
Her teeth can hardly stand,
She leaps — but robin leaps the first!
Ah, pussy of the sand,

The hopes so juicy ripening,
You almost bathed your tongue
When bliss dissolved a hundred wings
And fled with every one!

—EMILY DICKINSON

from *TO A CAT*

Stately, kindly, lordly friend
   Condescend
Here to sit by me, and turn
Glorious eyes that smile and burn.

Dogs may fawn on all and some
   As they come
You, a friend of loftier mind
Answer friends alone in kind
Just your foot upon my hand
Softly bids me understand.
   —ALGERNON CHARLES SWINBURNE

ODE TO A CAT

There is nothing quite so restful as a cat
When the weary day is ended
And your head is bowed and bended
Who is nicer to come home to than a cat?
Just like the peaceful waves upon a distant shore
Never yammering or yowling
Just a courteous meowing
When the little beastie greets you at the door.
Although a dog may be appealing
Firm and faithful in his dealing
All his love for you revealing
This won't change the way I feel
I'm standing pat, I like a cat
He is always welcome to my welcome mat.
No, there is nothing so relaxing as a cat
It's a pleasure to observe him
Nothing ever can unnerve him
With a cat you know exactly where you're at
No, there's nothing quite so restful as a cat.

—HERBERT B. GREENHOUSE

GOOD-TIME CHARLIE

"Good-Time Charlie" was a city cat.
He lived in Greenwich Village with his mistress,
Vivian Cristol. Here she reveals Charlie's
independent personality.

Some years ago, a gentleman caller in a fit of pique
said to me, "If I came on all fours and miaowed
outside your door, I'll bet you'd be a hell of a lot
nicer to me than you are." Yes, such a metamor-
phosis would certainly have improved his chances.
And he might have become involved with me far
far more than he had in mind!

For to me, letting even a cat into your life is no
casual affair but a real commitment. They will im-
pinge on your freedom and mobility. You cannot
with honor divorce or abandon them. You grow to
love them, and loving makes you vulnerable.

Charlie is my second cat, the cat that came after
the cat I dearly loved. I wasn't ready to love another cat. Charlie was even warier: to him, there
was safety only in numbers . . . .

Every day, I might add, Charlie repays my in-
vestment in him. He continually delights my eye,
frequently amuses me, and often touches my heart-
strings. He never bores me. His joy in nature re-

news my own, his independence reinforces mine. And in his fashion I know he will love me in December as he did in May.

Despite his charm and good looks, had I known his true personality in the beginning I wonder if I would have been so hell-bent to have him. Or put up with all his humiliating nonsense. Even now, after five years, he's insecure. Self-involved. Obdurate. Always for the status quo, whatever the choice. Undemonstrative, unless he's sick or tired, the weather's bad, or there's nothing to do. Totally predictable. Were he a man, he'd be the kind who'd read the newspaper at the breakfast table, sports section and comics first, and spend his evenings with television or the boys. Not my type at all.

By now, though, we've been through so much together that I love him. And what love couldn't accomplish, habit, comfort, and relative affluence have, so that he is no longer quite so free and easy as in those early days. This is the way it usually works, as any patient woman can tell you. Unwittingly he became my responsibility. He came into my life off his feed and off guard. The overtures were all mine. Nothing was conditional. So, like the bride whose husband chased her until she caught him, I was stuck with his shortcomings.

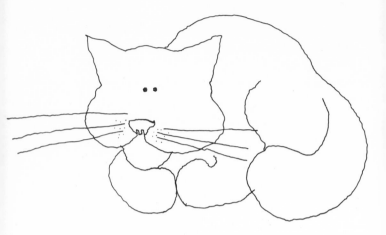

The trouble with a kitten is that
Eventually it becomes a cat!

—OGDEN NASH

Cat, n. A soft, indestructible automaton provided
by nature to be kicked when things go wrong in
the domestic circle.

—AMBROSE BIERCE

Cats are rather delicate creatures and they are
subject to a good many different ailments, but I
never heard of one who suffered from insomnia.

—JOSEPH WOOD KRUTCH

Cats like to sleep soft.

—THEOCRITUS

Never wake a sleeping cat.
                    —FRANCOIS RABELAIS

Cats are like women, and women are like cats.
They are both very ungrateful.
                    —DAMON RUNYON

When I play with my cat, who knows but that she
regards me as a plaything even more than I do her?
                    —MICHEL DE MONTAIGNE

The cat in gloves catches no mice.
                    —BENJAMIN FRANKLIN

No matter how much cats fight, there always seem
to be plenty of kittens.
                    —ABRAHAM LINCOLN

If man could be crossed with the cat, it would im-
prove man, but it would deteriorate the cat.
                    —MARK TWAIN

Cats know how to obtain food without labor, shelter
without confinement, and love without penalties.
                    —W. L. GEORGE

A baited cat may grow as fierce as a lion.
                    —SAMUEL PALMER

In her book, Memoir for Mrs. Sullavan,
*Bryna Ivens Untermeyer delightfully describes
her cats' attraction to the mysterious plant, catnip.*

All the cats liked catnip, some more, some less, each reacting to it differently. Sullavan was particularly fond of catnip-stuffed toys; she would worry them frenetically, with an ardent tongue and eager claws, until she ripped them apart. Then she lost interest and left the catnip itself for me to clean up. To fresh or dried catnip served to her decorously in a dish, she reacted with adult decorum, eating a modest quantity appreciatively, never overdoing it or showing any undue effects.

Cleo, on the other hand, grew giddy on her first leaf, lost control with the second, and made a silly spectacle of herself with the third. She would eventually fall into her plate and squirm around on the floor, rubbing the catnip into her fur like a giggling girl on New Year's Eve showering herself with confetti.

Bobo was the heaviest imbiber of them all. He carried his catnip like a man, could consume a considerable quantity of it without any signs of intoxication, and then slept it off. If he didn't get his nip regularly, he missed it and asked for it.

In the early years, we had a metal breadbox that

stood on a counter in the kitchen, the kind that has a front flap hinged at the top. We never kept bread in it but an odd assortment of things, including the box or jar of catnip. Bobo learned to lift the metal flap, bang it up and down, and even, if it wasn't too far back, pull out the catnip. When we heard the metal clanging, we knew Bobo wanted to go on a binge. Eventually, as the kitchen underwent alterations, with new cabinets and counters installed, the breadbox was discarded. After that we kept the catnip with the cat foods, on one of the upper shelves of the supply closet behind the kitchen door, a fairly inaccessible full-length closet. The new cabinet doors were wood; they didn't lock, but were of the type that pushed shut, and did not shut tight. It soon became apparent that Bobo could hook a claw under one of these and pull it open. Slow-witted that we were, we wondered why he kept working on these doors, not only opening them one after another but pushing them closed again. It was a nuisance — until it dawned on us that he was translating his "Catnip, please" into new terms. There was no question that this was what he was trying to say. As soon as we caught on and served him his ration, he was satisfied. Then he would leave the cupboard doors alone until the next time he felt like indulging.

THE FIRESIDE SPHINX

Half loving-kindliness and half disdain,
    Thou comest to my call serenely suave,
With humming speech and gracious gestures
      grave,
    In salutation courtly and urbane:

Yet must I humble me thy grace to gain —
    For wiles may win thee, but no arts enslave,
    And nowhere gladly thou abidest save
Where naught disturbs the concord of thy reign.

Sphinx of my quiet hearth! who deignst to dwell
    Friend of my toil, companion of mine ease,
    Thine is the lore of Ra and Rameses;
That men forget dost thou remember well,
    Beholden still in blinking reveries,
    With sombre sea-green gaze inscrutable.

                      —GRAHAM R. THOMSON

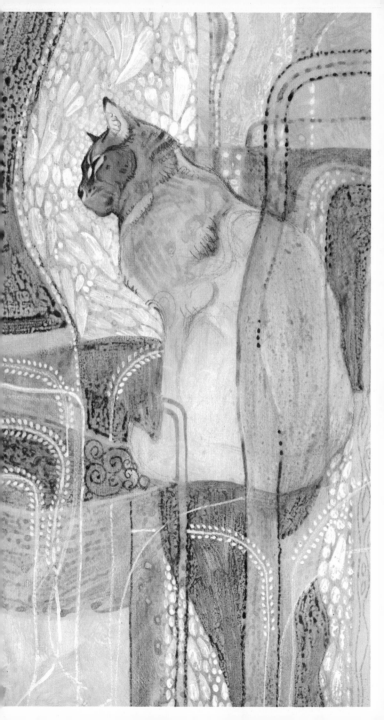

A FRIEND INDEED

*Securing the friendship of a cat
is not an easy matter. Théophile Gautier,
a French author and cat fancier,
explains the cat-human relationship
and the comfort derived from it.*

. . . The cat is a philosophical, methodical, quiet animal, tenacious of his own habits, fond of order and cleanliness, and does not lightly confer his friendship. If you are worthy of his affection, a cat will be your friend but never your slave. He makes himself the companion of your hours of solitude, melancholy and toil. He will remain for whole evenings on your knee, uttering a contented purr, happy to be with you. Put him down and he will jump up again with a sort of cooing sound like a gentle reproach; and sometimes he will sit upon the carpet in front of you looking at you with eyes so melting, so caressing and so human, that they almost frighten you, for it is impossible to believe that a soul is not there.

THE CAT

The sleeping cat
begins to stir,
stretches her legs
in front of her . . .
opens her eyes
a narrow slit,
swishes her tail
and watches it . . .
Then up she gets
on velvet paws,
arches her back,
opens her jaws . . .
then breathing one
long boring sigh,
away she pads
with tail held high.

—ALICE CAROLINE SMITH

I LOVE 'EM

Cats are, of course, no good. They're chiselers and panhandlers, sharpers and shameless flatterers. They're as full of schemes and plans, plots and counterplots, wiles and guiles as any confidence man. They can read your character better than a $50-an-hour psychiatrist. They know to a milligram how much of the old oil to pour on to break you down. They are definitely smarter than I am, which is one reason why I love 'em.

—PAUL GALLICO

THIS MUFF OF FUR

The glossy brute
Fears not one hoot
My lame pursuit,
And every night
Sneaks out to fight,
Seduce, and prowl;
Long after three,
I hear him yowl
To waken me;
Dizzy with sin,
He staggers in.
　　Damn his black skin.
In my castle
He is the king
And I his vassal.
Bound to appease,
Beseeching paws
With indrawn claws
Pad my old knees;
He knows how weak
I am — the sneak,
Softer than silk
Close by my side,
Milder than milk.
　　Bless his black hide.

—MILDRED R. HOWLAND

53

KITTENS

See the kitten on the wall,
Sporting with the leaves that fall . . . .
But the kitten, how she starts,
Crouches, stretches, paws and darts
First at one and then its fellow,
Just as light and just as yellow:
There are many now — now one,
Now they stop, and there are none.
What intenseness of desire
In her upward eye of fire.
With a tiger-leap halfway
Now she meets the coming prey,
Lets it go as fast, and then
Has it in her power again:
Were her antics played in the eye
Of a thousand standers-by,
Clapping hands with shout and stare,
What would little Tabby care
For the plaudits of the crowd?
Over happy to be proud,
Over wealthy in the treasure
Of her own exceeding pleasure.

              —WILLIAM WORDSWORTH

JUST CATS

People say that cats and women waste more time over their toilet than any other creatures . . . If the old precept Cleanliness is next to Godliness still demands respect, then cats must be ranked very high in their approach to Godliness. Higher in fact than the human race . . . How characteristic of cats is the movement with which it can turn and lick the very middle of its back; and then pause with the twist still in its body and look at you, as if to demonstrate the very ease with which it does it.

—T. O. BEACHCROFT

A CAT

Philosopher and comrade, not for thee
The fond and foolish love which binds the dog;
Only a quiet sympathy which sees
Through all my faults and bears with them awhile..
Be lenient still, and have some faith in me,
Gentlest of skeptics, sleepiest of friends.

—JULES LEMAITRE

A LITERARY POINT OF VIEW
The cat has often been considered an inspiration
to authors and poets.
His grace, mysticism and symmetry urge
one to achieve
an equally perfect form.
In the book Tiger in the House,
Carl Van Vechten talks about literary men
who have loved cats .

Even in the dark ages the cat was the friend of the intelligent man, for the sorcerers and alchemists were the philosophers of the period and those who persecuted sorcerers and cats were the philistines. In our day the cat is as essential to the literary workshop as he was formerly to the alchemystical laboratory. French writers, especially, have made a fetish of the soft and independent little fellow animal. Hardly an author of distinction during the nineteenth century in Paris who did not surround himself with harems of long-haired Persian beauties. Prosper Mérimée, Théophile Gautier, Victor Hugo, Charles Baudelaire, Paul de Kock, André Theuriet, Émile Zola, Joris Karl Huysmans, Jules Lemaître, Pierre Loti, Octave Mirbeau, and Anatole France all loved cats. Those in this list who are yet alive still do love them. Maupassant stands out as a solitary figure opposed to the cult, for I gather from his rather unsympathetic essay on cats that he neither understood nor cared for them. The others revived cat-worship, for which there are sufficient reasons. Dogs are noisy, restless, clumsy, and dirty. As W. H. Hudson has remarked they are useful and therefore should be relegated with other useful animals to their proper place in the stables and the fields. Two or three dogs about the house are sufficient to distract the attention and to claim one's time, but it is possible to endure, nay to enjoy, the companionship of seventeen or more pussies, especially if they are aristocratic pussies. They keep themselves faultlessly clean and have no odour. They walk about noiselessly. Persian cats seldom mew and when they do their voices are modulated like those of well-bred people. They offer a pleasing exterior to the eye; their velvet backs invite caresses. When a man is tired a cat does not excite his nerves; when he is rested he can turn to puss for play . . . .

It is perfectly possible (a fact which I have proved scores of times myself) to work not only with a cat in the room, but with a cat on one's shoulder or in one's lap. In a draughty room, indeed, the cat makes a superior kind of paper-weight! Cats, to be sure, love to play on tables with loose papers and pens, but a little care will keep them from doing damage, and how welcome is the soft paw tap on the pen with the look of surprise that invariably follows, to the tired writer.

As an inspiration to the author I do not think the cat can be over-estimated. He suggests so much grace, power, beauty, motion, mysticism. The perfect symmetry of his body urges one to achieve an equally perfect form. His colour and his line alone would serve to give any imaginative creator material for several pages of nervous description; on any subject, mind you, not necessarily on the cat himself. As for his intelligence, his occult power, they are so remarkable that I sometimes feel convinced that true cat-lover authors are indebted even more deeply than they believe to "cats of ebony, cats of flame" for their books. The sharp, but concealed claws, the contracting pupil of the eye, which allows only the necessary amount of light to enter, the independence, should be the best of models for any critic; the graceful movements of the animal who waves a glorious banner as he walks silently should stir the soul of any poet. The cat symbolizes, indeed, all that a good writer tries to put into his work. I do not wonder that some writers love cats; I am only surprised that all writers do not love cats.

THE LESSON

You may have noticed, little friends,
That cats don't wash their faces
Before they eat, as children do
In all good Christian places.

Well, years ago, a famous cat
The pangs of hunger feeling,
Had chanced to catch a fine young mouse,
Who said, as he ceased squealing:

'All genteel folk their faces wash
Before they think of eating.'
And, wishing to be thought well-bred,
Puss heeded his entreating.

But when she raised her paw to wash,
Chance for escape affording,
The sly young mouse said his goodbye,
Without respect to wording.

A feline council met that day,
And passed, in solemn meeting,
A law forbidding any cat
To wash till *after* eating.

—AUTHOR UNKNOWN

EPITAPH

Bathsheba: —
To whom none ever said scat.
No worthier cat
Ever sat on a mat
Or caught a rat: —
  Requies-cat.

—JOHN GREENLEAF WHITTIER

Set at The Castle Press in Intertype Walbaum, a light, open typeface designed by Justus Erich Walbaum (1768-1839), who was a typefounder at Goslar and at Weimar. Printed on Hallmark Eggshell Book paper. Designed by S. Louise Howey.